THE
WISDOM
of JESUS

KENNETH SCHENCK

wphonline.com

Copyright © 2014 by Kenneth Schenck
Published by Wesleyan Publishing House
Indianapolis, Indiana 46250
Printed in the United States of America
ISBN: 978-0-89827-739-5
ISBN (e-book): 978-0-89827-816-3

Library of Congress Cataloging-in-Publication Data

Schenck, Kenneth, 1966- author.
  The wisdom of Jesus / Kenneth Schenck.
    pages cm
  ISBN 978-0-89827-739-5 (pbk.) -- ISBN 978-0-89827-816-3
(e-book) 1. Sermon on the mount. I. Title.
  BT380.3.S34 2014
  226.9'06--dc23

                              2014007129

All Scripture quotations, unless otherwise indicated, are taken from
the Holy Bible, New International Version®, NIV ®. Copyright
©1973, 1978, 1984, 2011 by Biblica, Inc. Used by permission of
Zondervan. All rights reserved worldwide. www.zondervan.com. The
"NIV" and "New International Version" are trademarks registered in
the United States Patent and Trademark Office by Biblica, Inc.

Scripture quotations marked (KJV) are taken from the HOLY BIBLE, KING
JAMES VERSION.

All rights reserved. No part of this publication may be reproduced,
stored in a retrieval system, or transmitted in any form or by any
means—electronic, mechanical, photocopy, recording or any other—
except for brief quotations in printed reviews, without the prior written
permission of the publisher.

CONTENTS

For a free download of group study and sermon notes, visit
www.wphresources.com/wisdom.

INTRODUCTION

The Sermon on the Mount, Matthew 5–7, gives us some of Jesus' best known teaching. For example, it has the Beatitudes. It has Jesus' teaching on loving our enemy and turning the other cheek. In the Sermon on the Mount we find the Lord's Prayer, Jesus' teaching on not judging others, and much more. It is, in many respects, Jesus' earthly teaching in a nutshell, and Matthew may have meant for his listeners to see the sermon as a summary of Jesus' teaching.

In Matthew, Jesus gave the sermon on a mountain. Since one of the themes of the sermon is that Jesus came to fulfill the law, it is hard not to see a parallel with Moses here. God gave the law to Moses on Mount Sinai, so Jesus gave his followers the fulfilled law on a mountain as well. This is not the only echo of Moses in Matthew. The way Matthew tells the story of Jesus' birth would have made any Jew at the time think of Moses, from the killing of innocent children and Jesus' escape, to Jesus leaving Egypt. And the book of Matthew itself can be divided into five parts, just like the five books of Moses that begin the Old Testament.

Although the gospel of Matthew is technically anonymous, it has always been associated with Matthew the tax collector (compare Matt. 9:9–13). It came to be called a "gospel" because it relayed the good news of how Jesus became king. Matthew is the most Jewish gospel in flavor, and he likely wrote for a Christian Jewish audience. Of all the Gospels, therefore, Matthew's audience probably came closest to Jesus' original audience.

This book presents six weeks of Bible studies on the Sermon on the Mount. Each week looks at a different part of the sermon, covering roughly a half chapter each week. Each week contains five days of reflection on the text and examines only a few verses each day. Our aim is to experience life transformation by hearing God speak to us through the words Jesus spoke to the crowds and that Matthew then passed on to his first-century audience. We want to hear God speak to us through Scripture and then live faithfully to his Word through the power of the Holy Spirit.

The first two weeks look at Matthew 5, which begins with the Beatitudes and ends with Jesus showing us what it means to live out the fulfilled law of the Old Testament. The second two weeks then work through Matthew 6, in which Jesus explained what true righteousness looks like, a righteousness not like that of the scribes or the stereotypical Pharisee. Surpassing righteousness does not focus on the earthly or what others think, but on God. Finally, the last two weeks look at Matthew 7, where Jesus wrapped up his teaching and gave warnings to us as we build our spiritual houses.

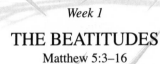

Week 1

THE BEATITUDES

Matthew 5:3–16

Let your light shine before others, that they may see your
good deeds and glorify your Father in heaven.

—Matthew 5:16

Day 1

POOR IN SPIRIT
Matthew 5:3–6

INTRODUCTION

The first verses of the Sermon on the Mount are called the Beatitudes, the "blesseds," and are some of Jesus' most famous teaching. They set the tone for the whole sermon with a celebration of the honor of those who serve God despite earthly hardship.

ENGAGE

The first four beatitudes celebrate the poor in spirit, those who hunger for righteousness, those who mourn now, and those who are meek. Being poor in spirit means having a spirit of dependence on God, regardless of what earthly possessions you might have. It is a realization that you are not sufficient to make it on your own and must rely on God. Those who hunger for righteousness are also blessed and yearn to live in a way pleasing to God. Those who mourn now will find themselves at rest in the kingdom. Their current troubles will soon come to an end. Meanwhile, the meek do not promote themselves and, in this world, are usually overlooked. In the kingdom, God will give them the earth.

Every good and perfect gift is from above,
coming down from the Father of the heavenly
lights, who does not change like shifting shadows.

—JAMES 1:17

EXAMINE

It may be hard for us to get a good sense of what Jesus meant by being blessed. Our first instinct is probably to think it means being happy. We think in terms of happiness because Western culture is so individual-oriented, and it is hard for us to get our minds around what a group-oriented or honor-shame culture looks like. In Jesus' world, being blessed was honor language. Honored are the poor in spirit. Honored are they who mourn.

Honored are the meek. These individuals, who are dishonored now on earth, are greatly honored in God's eyes now and will receive great honor in the coming kingdom. Meanwhile, those who are honored now will find their fortunes reversed then.

EXPLORE

The values of the kingdom do not come naturally. We are programmed to yearn for the success story and to assert ourselves. We admire the "self-made" man or woman who is self-reliant, not the meek. We hunger for success and worldly approval. But Jesus honors the poor in spirit, the person who has an attitude of dependence on God. Jesus honors the person who hungers to do what is right, not to succeed. Is it possible to be a "doer" who realizes that God gives the increase? We are so prone to give ourselves credit for what looks like success. Can we be assertive for God's mission because we know he is with us? Can we be meek toward ourselves, yet pushy for the kingdom?

PRAYER

Spirit, do a miracle in my heart, and help me to fully realize that you are the one bringing the increase in my life.

Day 2

PURE IN HEART
Matthew 5:7–9

INTRODUCTION

The next three beatitudes have to do with our hearts. The kind of person God honors is the person who is merciful and who facilitates peace between those in conflict. God especially values the person whose motives are pure.

ENGAGE

One of the key characteristics of God in both the Old and New Testaments is his mercy. God often does not give us the punishment we deserve. He expects no less of us. The parable of the unmerciful servant captures this dynamic so well (Matt. 18:21–35). A servant who owed his master an unbelievable amount was forgiven, but he

turned around and refused to forgive the debt of someone who owed him a paltry amount. When the master
found out, he "unforgave" the debt of the first servant.
The parable acts out for us in a negative way what the
beatitude puts positively. When we are merciful to others,
God delights in being merciful to us. When we are
unforgiving, God will not forgive us.

Purity of heart is to will one thing.

—Søren Kierkegaard

EXAMINE

Some people like to think of Jesus as a troublemaker.
They relish the picture of Jesus putting Pharisees in their
place or scolding self-righteous priests. They love the
picture of him overthrowing the tables of the money-
changers. They may want to see the sinner destroyed.
Civil religion in America sometimes equates patriotism
with godliness, to the point where those who question
going to war are almost considered immoral. Pacifists
are seen as liberals and therefore considered evil. But
Jesus said, "Blessed are the peacemakers." Blessed are

those who avert conflict, not those who relish it. Honored are those who reconcile those at war. More blessed are those who broker peace than those who enforce justice by war.

EXPLORE

What does it mean to be pure in heart? It means for our intentions to be pure. It means that we serve others truly to serve others, not to advance ourselves. It means we do not act from hidden agendas that are meant to serve only ourselves. As human beings, we will never be free of temptation. Our bodies have desires and drives built in that will always make us have to choose. Purity of heart is more about a consistency in the choices we make than it is the conflicting feelings and temptations we face. By God's grace, we can be pure in heart because we are committed to doing the right thing in every choice we face.

PRAYER

Jesus, keep me from having a skewed picture in my head of who you are, but help me see who you really are, an agent of peace.

Day 3

THE PERSECUTED
Matthew 5:10–12

INTRODUCTION

Most of the first seven beatitudes might in theory apply to anyone. These verses turn to those who are explicitly persecuted because they are doing the right thing. The reversal of their fortunes will be particularly striking.

ENGAGE

Something about human nature can lead us to insult or attack those who are better than us. An honest person can inadvertently make a liar feel guilty. A hard worker can make a lazy person feel guilty. The guilty or intimidated person sometimes attacks the other, not only with insults but with violence. At other times, an unrighteous person may need you to look the other way for their plans to work. The person wanting to do what is right can stand in the way of those who want to do evil. Whatever the reason, it has often been the case that a person wanting to do what is right undergoes persecution from others. Jesus gives hope in such cases—God will vindicate the righteous.

The blood of the martyrs is the seed of the church.

—TERTULLIAN

EXAMINE

When we hear that someone's reward is great in heaven, we might think about going to heaven when we die. But Matthew 8:11 indicates that the feast of the kingdom will be on earth, and there is good reason to believe that the New Testament writers expected a renewed earth (for example, Rom. 8:21). So when Jesus said that great is the reward of the persecuted in heaven, he was probably referring to the place from which the reward comes, not to heaven as the place where we go in some next life. Similarly, the phrase "the kingdom of heaven" in Matthew probably does not mean that the kingdom of God will be in heaven but that heaven is the place from which God rules as king.

EXPLORE

It is so easy to mistake our personality for the "right way." So there is a certain personality that almost longs to be a martyr. It reads verses about persecution and almost desires it. "If you're not suffering for the Lord," someone might say, "you're doing something wrong." But this is the wrong approach. The question is whether we are doing the right thing. Sometimes, we will experience persecution for doing the right thing. Sometimes, by God's grace, we will not. Sometimes a person can even be honored for doing the right thing, even by the world. Do not seek conflict with the world. But do what God wants you to do, even if you know it will result in hardship.

PRAYER

Father, I trust in your promise and, by your power, commit to do what is right regardless of the consequences.

Day 4

TASTING SALTY
Matthew 5:13

INTRODUCTION

In between the Beatitudes and Jesus' teaching on fulfilling the law, we find two short comparisons of God's people to salt and light. In the first comparison, we learn that Christians should taste good.

ENGAGE

Salt has been used throughout history to preserve food. The version of this saying in Mark 9:50 may indeed have the sense that Christians should live as salt among each other, a force that preserves the body and fosters peace among themselves. The opposite would be for Christians to cause each other to spoil. But the saying in Matthew seems to focus on salt as something that makes food taste better. As we live in the world, we should make the world a better place. And, of course, we should keep the world from spoiling too. We should be attractive to others, not because we are conforming to the ways of the world but because we genuinely taste good.

Everyone will be salted with fire. Salt is good, but if it loses its saltiness, how can you make it salty again? Have salt among yourselves, and be at peace with each other.

—MARK 9:49–50

EXAMINE

A chemistry professor of mine once mused on the notion of salt losing its saltiness. Technically speaking, the atoms in salt will always be the same atoms. But what can happen is that the thing you think is salt no longer actually has any salt in it. Jesus was using ordinary language. Galileans no doubt understood what "salt gone bad" was like. It was never to be salty again—we know, because it had ceased being salt. It was useless, something to throw out. A Christian that does not taste good and is not a force for good may not actually be a Christian any longer. He or she has become something else. Thankfully, God always takes back prodigals.

EXPLORE

Salt makes food taste better. It always has, because of the way our tongues work. Of course, Jesus' saying is a proverb. It does not work all the time. Sometimes doing right ends up in persecution, as the previous verses tell us. But at other times, doing the right thing can draw others to Christ. Christians should not be hard to get along with. We should not have a bitter taste. And we should be a force that slows down the rotting of the world. Does the world around us become more loving simply because of our presence? If not, we should ask ourselves some serious questions and pray to the God who can make salt out of nothing.

PRAYER

Father, turn me into salt that promotes righteousness and makes you taste good to the world around me.

Day 5

LIGHT THAT SHINES
Matthew 5:14–16

INTRODUCTION

Jesus followed his comparison of God's people to salt with a comparison of them to light. As we are to be salt in the world, so we are to be light.

ENGAGE

The purpose of light is to help us see in the dark. The good Christians do is supposed to be that sort of light to the world. Jesus was of course speaking in metaphors, making comparisons to help the crowds understand deep truths. Perhaps a mirror would be an even closer metaphor than a light. The light people see in us is the light of Christ that we reflect to them. At the same time, the purpose of our light is not to draw attention to us, but to glorify our

Father in heaven. It is a light God shares with us and a light we share with others. May our lives shine forth!

EXAMINE

We have to balance what Jesus said about showing the world our good deeds with what he said in the next chapter about not showing off our good deeds. The point here is not showing them off, but having good deeds to show. This idea does not sit well with the current climate, which emphasizes that all of us are imperfect. Anyone who would claim to be a moral example today would inevitably sound like a hypocrite. But Paul himself told his churches several times to follow his example (see Phil. 3:17)—he apparently had not heard that we could never be righteous in this life. The New Testament is not against good deeds. God expects us to produce good deeds.

EXPLORE

As Christians, we are cities on a hill. People can see us. Perhaps a more contemporary example would be a skyline like that of New York City or Chicago. You can see the city from miles away because of how tall the skyscrapers are. People are watching us. What are they seeing? Are they seeing a light to show the way? If you have ever been in a blackout, you know how comforting it is to have a flashlight that works. If we are living as light to the world, people will make unexpected comments to us. Hopefully, we will be a little surprised at the compliments because we were just being ourselves in Christ. We will have followers without knowing it.

PRAYER

Jesus, may others be able to find you by walking in the footprints I am leaving behind.

How far that little candle throws his beams!
So shines a good deed in a weary world.

—WILLIAM SHAKESPEARE

BRIDGING JESUS' WORLD AND OURS

The Beatitudes are all about the reversal of values that takes place in the kingdom. Those who mourn now will rejoice then. Those who are persecuted now will rule then. The poor now will possess then. The last two thousand years have included times and places where Christians have suffered, as well as instances where they had easy lives. We normally do not get to choose which kind of context we get.

We must be faithful servants to the Lord no matter what setting we inherit. We must be poor in spirit whether or not we are poor in our bank accounts. We must hunger and thirst for righteousness whether our stomachs are full or empty. We must be salt and light in the world whether our world is cloudy or bright. God will be faithful to us no matter the context. So also we must be faithful to him regardless of our circumstances.

EXERCISE

In all your dealings with others this week, ask yourself whether their encounters with you are more likely to attract them to Christ or drive them away from him. Are you salt and light in your world or do you leave a bitter taste toward Jesus?

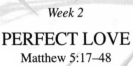

Week 2

PERFECT LOVE
Matthew 5:17–48

If you love those who love you, what reward
will you get? . . . Be perfect, therefore,
as your heavenly Father is perfect.

—MATTHEW 5:46, 48

Day 1

SUPERIOR RIGHTEOUSNESS
Matthew 5:17–20

INTRODUCTION

These verses are arguably the key verses of the Sermon on the Mount. The rest of the sermon plays out how the law is truly fulfilled and what a righteousness superior to that of the teachers of the law and Pharisees actually looks like.

ENGAGE

We might think at first that Jesus not only wants us to continue to keep even the smallest commandments of the Old Testament (like not trimming beards) but that he was making the law even harder. The rest of Matthew 5, however, makes it clear that Jesus' "fulfilled" reading of the law filters it significantly. Jesus passed the law through the love principle, and the result was that some Old Testament laws became more intense, while others fell away. Now not only can you not murder, you cannot even hate. But the "eye for an eye" command fell away, because it does not fit the principle of loving your enemy. It is the *heart* of the "smallest letter" that does not fall away.

Deep within our conscience we discover a law
that we have not laid upon ourselves but that
we must obey. Its voice, ever calling us to love and
to do what is good and to avoid evil, sounds
in our hearts at the right moment.

—PARAPHRASE OF THE ROMAN CATHOLIC CATECHISM

EXAMINE

The "Law and the Prophets" was a shorthand for the whole Old Testament. Jews both then and now divide the Old Testament into three sections: the Law (first five books), the Prophets (which included historical books like Joshua), and the Writings (chief of which was the Psalms). So the Sermon on the Mount is not just giving Jesus' fulfilled application of the Jewish Law. It is talking about a fulfilled understanding of Scripture itself as a whole, remembering that there was no New Testament yet. The "Law and the Prophets" were the Scriptures Jesus and Paul used. Jesus and Paul both saw their teaching in complete continuity with the Old Testament, especially when it was properly and spiritually understood.

EXPLORE

The idea that one's righteousness would need to be greater than that of Pharisees no doubt would have struck terror into the hearts of Jesus' audiences. While we are programmed to think of Pharisees as unrighteous hypocrites today, the Jews thought of Pharisees as perhaps the most righteous people around. After all, didn't the Pharisees follow a very strict lifestyle in what they did, who they associated with, and even what they ate? But Matthew 5:20 anticipates what Jesus would spell out in greater detail in Matthew 6. True righteousness is a matter of our hearts and a true desire to serve God. The stereotypical Pharisee, by contrast, was more interested in getting praise from those around him.

PRAYER

Spirit, teach me what the real heart of serving God is about, and take away any misconceptions I may have.

Day 2

NO HATRED
Matthew 5:21–26

INTRODUCTION

The rest of Matthew 5 plays out Jesus' fulfilled application of the law to a number of Old Testament commands. The first has to do with the command not to murder.

ENGAGE

Jesus' teaching in Matthew 5 is not really about deepening Old Testament commands. It would be more accurate to say that Jesus gets to the heart of each command. So the heart of the commandment not to murder is not really about the external act. Certainly the external act is horrible, because it results in the loss of life. But the core of the wrong is in the heart of the murderer rather than in the act of murder itself. In that sense, anyone who hates other people is a murderer in his or her heart. And we are not talking here so much about the *feeling* of hatred but the mental *act* of feeding hatred, which of course can lead to the external act of murder.

Anyone who hates a brother or sister is a murderer, and you know that no murderer has eternal life residing in him.

—1 JOHN 3:15

EXAMINE

Tucked into Jesus' teaching on hatred and reconciliation is a curious paragraph on living in a hostile world where your enemies have the power to take you to court (Matt. 5:25–26). The situation seems to be one where you owe a debt to a nonbelieving enemy. Jesus' practical advice is to do what you can to stay on your enemy's good side. Many Christians today like to think of the Bible as giving absolute principles. They might see Christian life as living out ideals. But most of the Bible is very down to earth, pragmatic rather than idealistic. This paragraph is just one example of using common sense when you live among enemies who have the power to make your life difficult.

EXPLORE

What does it look like, not hating your enemies? It means more than refusing to stew when you are driving down the road thinking about them. It means you try your best to reconcile with them. Jesus taught here that our hatred toward others quickly becomes an obstacle to our relationship with God. How can we expect to find mercy with God if we do not show mercy to those who need our earthly forgiveness? To be sure, we cannot force others to reconcile with us. We can only do the best we can. We go to those with whom we are at odds. We make amends if we can. We resolve to act lovingly toward them, despite any feelings to the contrary.

PRAYER

Spirit, empower me to act in love toward others even when my feelings tell me I do not like them.

Day 3

MARITAL FAITHFULNESS
Matthew 5:27–32

INTRODUCTION

After discussing murder and hate, Jesus played out the fulfilled application of the law in relation to marriage. He not only deepened the meaning of marital faithfulness, he also showed its implications in terms of divorce.

ENGAGE

The heart of the command not to commit adultery is not merely about not sleeping with someone else's spouse. It means that you do not mentally sleep with another person. It means that you do not dream of being in a situation where it "accidentally" happens. It means that you go far beyond simply not doing wrong; you do not put yourself in situations where you are tempted to do wrong. Fulfilling the law is not just about actions. It is even more about our intentions as they lead to action. Additionally, this is not really a statement about our feelings. It is about feeding our feelings and hopes. It is about the way we have been training our minds long before an opportunity presents itself.

Faithfulness is not doing something right once but doing something right over and over and over and over.

—JOYCE MEYER

EXAMINE

Jesus' prohibition of divorce went along with his teaching on adultery. Divorce, as it were, is legally permitted adultery. To be sure, Jesus regularly taught about making exceptions in various situations. People always trumped the law. It would be deeply ironic if we took a rule and implemented it like the stereotypical Pharisees did—the opposite of Jesus' intent. Surely Jesus was here targeting the man who wants to commit adultery and divorces his wife to get around the rules. Surely at the root of Jesus' command is his typical compassion, not a hidden bent toward legalism that only peeks out here. He has in mind people, both men and women, who are using the letter of the law to get around its heart.

EXPLORE

We have still not caught the heart of Jesus if we continue to think of his teaching on adultery and divorce in terms of prohibitions, things we cannot do. Our goal should ultimately focus on the positive—to *do* righteous things. Part of being righteous is certainly not doing certain things. But how much richer to focus on doing *good* things! It is true that we should not lust after people to whom we are not married. How much better to look at your own spouse with longing! How much better to love your own spouse than just to avoid looking at other people's spouses! Rather than seeing how close to evil we can get, we should head consistently for the good.

PRAYER

Father, give me so much love for my life-mate that I do not ever need to be reminded of your teaching on adultery.

Day 4

REDIRECTING LAW
Matthew 5:33–42

INTRODUCTION

In the previous two passages, Jesus got to the heart of the matter in a way that took the commandment to the next level. In the two examples from today's verses, the heart of the matter significantly filters the Old Testament law.

ENGAGE

The commandment not to take God's name in vain had to do with oath taking. If you invoke God's name in an oath, you had better keep it. The story of Jephthah is an example of a bad vow that an Israelite still went on to keep (Judg. 11). Jesus redirected this one of the Ten Commandments. How about not taking oaths at all? If you are an honest person, people will trust your word without you needing to swear or take an oath. Like Jesus' teaching on murder and adultery, he got to the heart of the matter. Truthfulness is not just about keeping oaths. It is about having a truthful heart. We should be people who can be trusted.

Hate cannot drive out hate: only love can do that.

—MARTIN LUTHER KING, JR.

EXAMINE

Jesus' next teaching went even further in filtering the law. Perhaps originally the "eye for an eye" rule was meant to keep someone from taking two eyes in revenge for someone who took only one. Deuteronomy 19:21 though, does not word it that way. "Show no pity," it says. Deuteronomy was of course to be read in the context of civil law and running a society. There is still a place for governments to administer justice (for example, Rom. 13:4). But as individuals, Jesus said, we are not to seek revenge. In fact, we are to cooperate with our oppressors. In an oppressive context, the rest of the New Testament indicates, we are to leave justice to

God: "'I will repay,' says the LORD" (Rom. 12:19; Deut. 32:35).

EXPLORE

It is so easy to make excuses, especially to this sort of teaching: "I know Jesus said to turn the other cheek, *but* . . ."; "I know Jesus said to give your shirt as well as your jacket, *but* . . ." Perhaps Jesus *was* exaggerating a little, using hyperbole. Some even suggest that these reactions were meant to shame the oppressor. But most of us could bear a little extra time with the shocking things Jesus said. We want the "but" too much. We are too prone to treat the "turn the other cheek" part as the exception rather than the rule. We should cry out at the oppression done to others. Jesus bids us be willing to endure a bit longer when we are the target.

PRAYER

Jesus, in my feeble moments of suffering, help me keep in mind what you endured from sinners, and be thankful.

Day 5

LOVE YOUR ENEMY
Matthew 5:43–48

INTRODUCTION

This paragraph captures the essence of all the contrasts Jesus had made up to this point. It is a generalization of all the examples he gave of what it means to fulfill the Law and the Prophets. Love is the fulfillment.

ENGAGE

In Matthew 5:17, Jesus said he did not come to destroy the Law and the Prophets. In the verses that follow, he gave several examples of what he meant when he said he came instead to fulfill it. He went to the heart of the law, which is to love your neighbor. It is not merely about following the rules not to murder or commit adultery or keep your oaths. It is about reconciling. It is about loving your spouse. It is about being trustworthy. It is about loving your enemy as well as your neighbor. God is like that. God is "complete" or perfect in his love. He shows kindness not only to the righteous, but to the wicked as well.

EXAMINE

Most of us probably do not give a lot of thought to how we apply the Bible to our lives. Without even realizing it, many of us have grown up hearing pastors and teachers give us interpretations and ways of fitting different passages together. In this paragraph, Jesus gave us the key to applying not only the Old Testament, but the whole Bible to our lives. The key is that our hearts must be motivated by love. Any application of Scripture that involves hatred of other people is an illegitimate application. It is possible to keep the letter of the law with a heart that is in violation of it. This was the problem of the stereotypical Pharisee.

EXPLORE

Rain is a good thing if you live in a farming world; the sun too. God is a giver of good things. Amazingly, he not only gives good things to good people, he gives them to bad people as well. We are so prone to be nice to those who are nice to us, but to dish out meanness in return for meanness. Jesus pointed out this fact in this paragraph. If you are only good to those who do good to you, you are no better than many a wicked person. The word *perfect* is misleading. A better translation would be "complete." God goes the whole way and shows kindness to everyone. So we must go the whole way as well.

PRAYER

Spirit, give me the power to be like the Father in heaven, who shows love to everyone, not just those who serve him.

For the entire law is fulfilled in keeping this one command: "Love your neighbor as yourself."

—Galatians 5:14

BRIDGING JESUS' WORLD AND OURS

Jesus' words in Matthew 5 are just as timely today as ever. They give the most profound understanding of ethics we could have. It is not so much about what we do, although obviously what we do is important. It is why we do it. What are our motivations? At the center of what Jesus criticized in the Gospels is a lawyer-type approach that is so focused on the letter of the law that it misses the real point of the law.

So it is not about whether a person has biblical grounds for divorce, for example. It is about why a person wants to get divorced in the first place. A person whose spouse abuses them is not a person seeking divorce for selfish reasons. So to forbid them on the basis of the Bible is to miss the dynamics of Jesus' teaching entirely. Jesus' very point is that we should live out of a heart that wants what is in the best interests of others.

EXERCISE

Examine yourself this week for the two extremes. Do you so pursue the letter of the law that you undermine the spirit of Jesus? On the other hand, do you understand the need for God's discipline as part of love, to steer you in the right direction?

Week 3

PRACTICING RIGHTEOUSNESS
Matthew 6:1–18

Be careful not to practice your righteousness in front
of others to be seen by them. If you do, you will
have no reward from your Father in heaven.

—MATTHEW 6:1

Day 1

GIVING IN SECRET
Matthew 6:1–4

INTRODUCTION

If most of Matthew 5 played out what it might mean to fulfill the law, Matthew 6 begins to demonstrate what it might mean for a person's righteousness to surpass the righteousness of the teachers of the law and of the Pharisees. For one thing, it is a righteousness done for God rather than for show.

ENGAGE

Matthew 6:1 is a general statement that captures the essence of almost the whole chapter. Unlike the stereotypical teacher of the law and Pharisee, we should not do acts of righteousness in order to be seen by others. Those who do this sort of thing lay up for themselves treasures on earth, so to speak. They are not oriented around heaven but around the earth and worldly honor. They are not the sort of people who will be blessed in the next life, unlike the meek and the poor in spirit. So while it is good to give to the needy, if you are doing it for show, you'll get your reward from the show. Those who give to give, though, will receive their honor from heaven.

If you do one good deed your reward usually is to be set to do another and harder and better one.

—C. S. LEWIS

EXAMINE

Sometimes it seems like we humans are built to go to extremes. So there are some who take comments about doing acts of righteousness in secret a little too far. What is important to God is not whether other people know the good you do but what your motivation is for doing it. If you did good purely to get a heavenly reward, you would still have a wrong attitude because you would do it for reward, not out of love of your neighbor. Similarly, just because someone finds out you have done good in the world does not mean that God will not give you a reward. The point is not in the finding out, but in why we are doing acts of righteousness.

EXPLORE

Some readers of Matthew 6 have trouble getting the apostle Paul out of their minds. They might try to reinterpret these verses to say that no human being can truly do acts of righteousness. But that is not what Jesus said. Without blinking an eye, he asserted that we could do good things in the world. Not only that, but Matthew insists that God's people will help others in need when we can. We do not do it for show. We do not do it for reward. We do it because, when we do it to the least of these, we do it for Christ (Matt. 25:40). And although we do not do it for reward, God will reward us.

PRAYER

Jesus, give me opportunities to help those in need. When you do, I will gladly serve others as you did when you were on earth.

Day 2

PRAYING IN SECRET
Matthew 6:5–8

INTRODUCTION

In the first paragraph of the chapter, Jesus talked about giving to the needy secretly rather than trumpeting your acts of righteousness publicly. In the second part of the chapter, he said similar things about praying.

ENGAGE

The idea of a prayer closet—a place where you can get alone with God and focus on him—comes from these verses. It can be so tempting to let others know we have a prayer closet, that we have a prayer list, that we have regular devotions. That drive for acknowledgment detracts from the benefit of prayer. Do we really believe we are praying to God? Even when we pray alone, we can be talking to ourselves. It might not dawn on us that we are talking to someone else, to God no less. But the benefit of prayer is not for God; it is for us. It does us no good to pray if we are not actually praying to God.

In prayer it is better to have a heart without words than words without a heart.

—JOHN BUNYAN

EXAMINE

Jesus even criticized pagan prayers in these verses, which were apparently known for mindless repetition. Some Protestants have of course used this verse to argue against Roman Catholic practices like praying the rosary or saying liturgy. The problem is not in the repetition, but in the mindlessness. It is not the volume of our words that makes prayer effective. After all, God knows what we need already, and he knows it more accurately than we do by far. We do not need to jump through hoops or perform rituals to convince him to respond. He only asks for the sincerity of our hearts and the trueness of our devotion. A silent prayer is enough for him, although saying it aloud sometimes can help us.

EXPLORE

Most Christians today would not be tempted to pray on street corners, but some Christians do pray for show, even today. You might begin to wonder whether they are talking to God or talking for the benefit of the people around them. The human heart is incredibly clever at showing off, sometimes without even fully realizing it. A person can even try to impress other believers with his or her humility. In some contexts, people can be proud of how plainly they dress: "Look at me; I do not wear any jewelry or makeup"; "Look, I go to church"; "Look, I protest the evils of our country." Beware of your motives, even for doing the right sorts of things!

PRAYER

Father, help my motivations to be pure, and when I pray, help me pray to you and not to others or myself!

Day 3

YOUR KINGDOM COME
Matthew 6:9–10

INTRODUCTION

Jesus went on to give a proper example of how to pray. The Lord's Prayer begins with praise to God and submission to his will.

ENGAGE

To say, "Hallowed be your name," is to say that God's name is holy. God is awesome, and we should not take him lightly. The Jewish tradition eventually would not even say his name at all. One of the Ten Commandments insists that Israelites keep any vow they say in God's name. Our God is an awesome God. He is the king. Yet at the same time, Jesus prayed to God as his Father. It probably goes a little too far to think of God as our "Daddy," an informal sense of dads that probably did not exist in the ancient world. Nevertheless, it was significant and striking for Jesus to teach his followers to think of God as their Father.

If we only had eyes to see and ears to hear and wits to understand, we would know that the Kingdom of God in the sense of holiness, goodness, beauty is as close as breathing and is crying out to be born both within ourselves and within the world.

—FREDERICK BUECHNER

EXAMINE

Hebrew poetry is based on what is called parallelism. One form of parallelism is when a second line repeats the same idea as the first in similar terms. The prayer lines, "Your kingdom come, your will be done," demonstrate this sort of synonymous parallelism. The second part repeats the basic sense of the first in different terms. So for God's kingdom to come is for his will to be done on earth as it is in heaven. The kingdom of God is about the rule of God, and it was a rule that was coming in force to the earth in Jesus' ministry, the beginning of setting the world right. God is the king who rules from heaven.

EXPLORE

King and Father—God is both. It is essential for us to embrace both roles. Because he is our king, we submit to God's will. We do what he wants and obey him. We do so not only in our individual lives, but also in the world. We work to bring the rest of the world into submission to him in the ways he wants us to. But because he is our Father, we know he is working everything together for good. His commands are not capricious. If he allows evil or suffering, we know it is because of some greater good, even if we cannot see it. We obey him because he is king. We trust him because he is Father.

PRAYER

Father, I trust you, knowing you intend my good. King, I submit to you because it is your due.

Day 4

DELIVERANCE
Matthew 6:11–15

INTRODUCTION

After adoration and submission, the Lord's Prayer turns to our needs and requests. Although Jesus briefly touched on the mundane need for food, the more important need has to do with our spiritual life.

ENGAGE

God cares for all our needs, not just the spiritual ones. He cares about our need to have food each day, our "daily bread." In Matthew 10:29, Jesus encouraged his disciples by reminding them that God even cares about sparrows. Not one of them dies without God caring. If we follow his example, we will not just be interested in getting the "spiritual side" of people right, although this area of our existence is clearly the most important. But God cares for people physically too, as Jesus demonstrated time and time again. He cares about people economically and relationally. He cares about us psychologically and socially. The Lord's Prayer shows us that he welcomes our asking him about any part of our lives.

Only those who try to resist temptation
know how strong it is. . . . That is why bad people,
in one sense, know very little about badness.

—C. S. LEWIS

EXAMINE

Matthew used the Greek word for "debts" in his version of the prayer. Luke 11:4 uses the word *sins*. Perhaps they are both translating the same underlying Aramaic word. It warns us that we probably should not go too far in equating sins with financial debts. "Forgive us our transgressions" is the sense. We do of course owe God everything, from our existence to our daily bread. We owe him for the forgiveness he gives us. And over and over again, we see that we must forgive others to receive God's forgiveness. It is the merciful who will receive mercy. It is those who forgive others who will themselves be forgiven. Seventy times seven, we are to forgive those who do us wrong.

EXPLORE

We learn from James 1:13 that God himself does not tempt us to do evil. Temptation can come from Satan and others. We can be tempted by our own sinful passions. We can even be tempted by our God-given drives to be fruitful and multiply. Perhaps Adam was tempted in this way. Whatever it means for God not to lead us into temptation, it is roughly the same as his delivering us from the Evil One, namely, Satan. Our problem, presumably, is not that God leads us to be tempted, but that we sometimes put ourselves into situations where we are tempted. Some of us get as close as we can to sin without actually crossing the line. This is not the Jesus way.

PRAYER

Spirit, deliver me, not only from the temptations of the Devil but from the temptations I bring upon myself.

Day 5

FASTING IN SECRET
Matthew 6:16–18

INTRODUCTION

After instructing his audience to help the needy and pray in secret, Jesus concluded by telling his audience to fast in secret. This instruction was for the person who likes for others to see him or her suffer for the Lord.

ENGAGE

Fasting is the practice of skipping a meal or several meals, often accompanied by prayer. Apparently, some religious leaders at the time of Jesus made a big show of their fasting. We know the stereotype—the people who do not seem to be looking at God at all in their spiritual practice. They are not looking at God but looking at you, hoping you will notice: "Look at how gaunt my face is.

Hear my stomach growling? I have not eaten all day because I am spiritual." Suffice it to say, these people will not get the benefit of fasting, but are more likely to hurt themselves spiritually. They have clouded their channel to God rather than cleared it.

EXAMINE

Fasting was a part of the worship of ancient Israel. The Day of Atonement, the one day a year when the high priest went into the Most Holy Place of the temple, was a day of fasting for Israel. Why do we do it? It is not because it has physical benefits, although it probably does give our bodies a helpful purging. But more significant is the fact that fasting seems to help us focus in prayer. It catches our attention by deviating from our norm. It reflects a level of seriousness that we can otherwise easily avoid, especially in the often comfortable lives of the West. It is a mental place that is even more powerful to us than a prayer closet alone.

EXPLORE

Some of us like others to see how successful we are: "Look how God has blessed me." But Jesus' comments on fasting warn us about trying to get earthly honor by letting others know how sacrificial we are: "Look at how I have suffered for the Lord!" This is the person who wants to be a martyr. Perhaps they want us to feel sorry for them: "Wow, look at how much work you did! Wow, look at how much time you put into this event!" But did anyone ask them to do that work or put in that time? There is no honor in suffering for the Lord when the Lord is not calling you to suffer. It should all be about God, not us.

PRAYER

Father, reveal to me my true heart—not only when I have others fooled, but especially when I have myself fooled.

If there is no element of asceticism in our lives, if we give free rein to the desires of the flesh . . . we shall find it hard to train for the service of Christ.

—DIETRICH BONHOEFFER

BRIDGING JESUS' WORLD AND OURS

The different ways of showing off our righteousness may change over time, but the human temptation to show off has remained the same. Some show off because of insecurity. They are so starved inside for affirmation that they desperately want others to see any good in them so they can hear words of approval. They cannot wait to have God's ultimate approval, and his approval now seems so abstract. They can hardly keep themselves from the immediate fix of others' praise.

Still others are convinced that they are superior to people around them. Perhaps they actually do amazing things. But such people cannot see how insignificant they are *next to God*. They are so focused on how much higher they are than those around them that they barely notice how high God is above them.

Whatever the cause, Jesus told us not to show off the acts of righteousness we do. He did not in any way deny that we can do acts of righteousness. He simply said that we must do such acts of prayer, giving, or fasting for God. If we want any praise that counts at all, we will look to God for it.

EXERCISE

Think over this past week. What acts of righteousness did you do? Did you pray? Did you fast? Did you give to others? Thank God for the opportunity if you did. Now absorb God's Word into your life. If you did nothing, do something. If you showed off, stop.

Week 4

TRUSTING THE MASTER
Matthew 6:19–34

Seek first his kingdom and his righteousness,
and all these things will be given to you as well.

—MATTHEW 6:33

Day 1

TREASURES THAT COUNT
Matthew 6:19–21

INTRODUCTION

The bottom line about those who do acts of righteousness for show is that they are more interested in getting treasures on earth than in acquiring treasures that will last for eternity. Those who do acts of righteousness for God store up treasures in a heavenly bank account.

ENGAGE

In the light of eternity, it is rather foolish that we would focus our energies on earthly treasures to the exclusion of heavenly ones. When we put a few decades next to infinity, the decades basically reduce to zero. A shiny car will eventually make its way to the junkyard. The nice new outfit will get stains and holes over time.

American culture is materialistic on a scale unknown in the history of the world. We want more and more and more, and we throw it all away just as quickly. We need these words of Jesus perhaps more now than at any other time. "Looking good" and having stuff is completely unimportant to God, even if it is one of our biggest pre-occupations today.

What comes into our minds when we think about
God is the most important thing about us.

—A. W. TOZER

EXAMINE

You may have heard the statement about people who are "so heavenly minded that they are no earthly good." I doubt this old adage applies to many people today. Yet because we human beings have a tendency to go to extremes, it is worth reminding ourselves that there are some tasks that God would have us do in this world. An old chorus caught the sentiment well: "We'll work till Jesus comes." Jesus' teaching was proverbial in nature, and it takes wisdom to know when to apply which parts. Most of us need to hear that our true treasures are not here on earth. A few of us need to hear that there are things we need to be doing here and now.

EXPLORE

Where is your heart? You can tell by what you focus your energies on. Where do you spend most of your time? What do you spend most of your money on? What are most of the things lying around your home? How do you evaluate others? Do you evaluate them by what they wear? By their shoes? By the car they drive or the home they live in? By the church they go to? By whether they wear a tie to church? These are all external things, not a matter of one's heart, one's true identity. They are all important in the world and in business. You have to pay some attention to them to survive in the world. They are completely unimportant to God.

PRAYER

Father, help me to see what is important to you in this world I live in and what is merely passing away.

Day 2

ONE MASTER
Matthew 6:22–24

INTRODUCTION

In their own way, these verses continue the theme of treasuring the things of heaven over the things of earth. The passage ends with Jesus giving his audience a choice between following their master in heaven or serving money on earth.

ENGAGE

Just as we are to lay up our treasures in heaven rather than on earth, we are to serve our master in heaven rather than money on earth. Israel at the time of Jesus was not primarily a place oriented around money and coinage but a farmer's world, where villages tried to be largely self-sufficient. Members of the village could farm and fish to provide food. Women in the village could make clothing. Enough was made to survive. The idea of storing up wealth in this world had a particular flavor of perversity. It pointed to someone who was especially selfish and self-centered, someone who likely accrued possessions off the backs of others. It was hard to fathom how such a person could be righteous.

Keep your lives free from the love of money and be
content with what you have, because God has said,
"Never will I leave you; never will I forsake you."

—HEBREWS 13:5

EXAMINE

God spoke to the people of the Bible in language they could understand. Sometimes, as hard as we try, it is hard to see how the language Jesus used fits our lives and experiences. What does it mean for the eyes to be the light of the body? Does this statement connect to having planks and specks in our eyes? Jesus seemed to say that we should look at the world with the right eyes, eyes that let the light in rather than the darkness. What we long for with our eyes affects the light inside us. The goal is to see the world as God sees it and to focus on the right things, to have clear eyes.

EXPLORE

Have you ever been in a situation where two "bosses" pulled on you in two different directions? Ultimately, you find yourself having to choose whose authority to follow. Jesus painted a picture of money and earthly treasures as competing authorities to God. Following God and treasuring the things of heaven tends to lead you in a different direction than treasuring the things of earth does. In such competitions, there is no question who must win. It may be possible for a person to have money and not be mastered by it, but Jesus generally considered it an unlikely outcome. It is far more likely for the person with material wealth to be mastered by his or her earthly treasures.

PRAYER

Spirit, do not let me be self-deceived. Clear my vision, so that my whole mind is full of light.

Day 3

DON'T WORRY!
Matthew 6:25–27

INTRODUCTION

Being earthly minded is not just a matter of worldly wealth. We can get so focused on our earthly needs that we demonstrate a lack of trust in God.

ENGAGE

The person who worries about what to eat or drink has a different kind of earthly focus than the person trying to store up material treasures. But, in a sense, this "worrying" person is still trusting more in the visible and the earthly than in God's ability to provide. God will make sure we have food. God will make sure we have drink. God will make sure we are clothed and protected from the elements. Absolutely we should take care of our own. Absolutely we should do what we can. But there is also the business of God's kingdom to be about, things to do for Christ. And we should not get so pre-occupied with the mundane things, like Martha did in Luke 10, that we miss the extraordinary.

Worry does not empty tomorrow of its sorrow,
it empties today of its strength.

—CORRIE TEN BOOM

EXAMINE

We can be thankful that Jesus mentioned God's love of birds in these words. God cares for the birds of the air. From time to time, Christians think that humanity alone is of interest to God. But this is a rather anemic understanding of God's relationship with his creation. Apparently, he even cares about the grass of the field (see Matt. 6:30). Although some mock the idea, the Bible resonates with those who believe we should be good stewards of God's creation. A healthy attention to God's creation is a far cry from nature worship, espe-cially if the opposing voice is about amassing wealth. It is deeply ironic that many Christians mock those with such values, when these values flow directly from Jesus' words.

EXPLORE

It is amazing that we humans worry so much about things we cannot change. To be sure, a little worry is healthy when we can actually do something to improve a situation. If you are having chest pains, it is good if you worry enough to see a doctor. And it is always good to pray, as long as we are not using it as a stall tactic. But many other times, we worry even though we have done everything that can be done. It is easy to say it when we are not in that situation, but we cannot change the outcome of a surgery, for example, by worrying. God asks us to trust him. He is in control and knows what he is doing.

PRAYER

Father, I rest in you, no matter the outcome, knowing that you are in control of everything.

Day 4

GOD'S CARE
Matthew 6:28–32

INTRODUCTION

Jesus continued his teaching on not worrying about the mundane needs of this world. Having already talked about not worrying about food and drink, in these verses he focused more on how we need not worry about clothing.

ENGAGE

From Jesus' perspective, the grass and the flowers were good examples of how God takes care of his creation. The fields get their clothing without anyone having to worry about them. How often do we lack faith? And yet most of us live in a world that provides so much more than people in other times and places have had. We have a "safety net" in Social Security and welfare programs. Yet we still lack faith! We have so much to thank God for. How many of us have ever not had something to wear? Yet how many of us have worried at some point about how we look! The worst most of us could imagine is more than enough.

It is an interesting question how far men would retain their relative rank if they were divested of their clothes.

—HENRY DAVID THOREAU

EXAMINE

It is a revealing thought to realize that God's creation is better clothed than the most prized outfit on a Paris runway. No earthly designer could match the patterns of the most Intelligent Designer. The clothing of King Solomon could not outshine the garments of creation. There might also be an allusion here to pagan feasts and festivals, where gluttony and frenzied drinking were part of the fare. What to eat? What to drink? What shall I wear to the party? These questions are not just the questions of an ancient feast. They are the questions of "pagan parties" today as well. Such things are ultimately trivial. God will provide what we need. The rest should not be a worry, but an enjoyment of his blessing.

EXPLORE

Some worry quite a bit about how their lawns and homes look: "The neighbors have mowed their yard, I had better do ours." "It's Saturday—time to dust the living room." "Cleanliness is next to godliness." It is fine to have a hobby, but some get obsessed with how their things look. To Jesus, such preoccupations were trivial at best and idolatrous at worst. God put flowers in the field just fine with no one worrying about them, and those were destined for burning. Similarly, any "adorning" of our houses, yards, or ourselves will quickly pass away. The best things to invest in are the things that will last forever. How silly to put the emphasis on something that will disappear in such a short time.

PRAYER

Spirit, open my eyes to how blessed I am. Help me see how rarely—if ever—I lack anything I truly need.

Day 5

FIRST THINGS FIRST
Matthew 6:33–34

INTRODUCTION

These two verses certainly have the feel of a conclusion to the verses we have looked at this week. The bottom line is to seek God's kingdom and its values first. God will take care of the rest.

ENGAGE

All of Matthew 6 thus far has been showing Jesus' audiences what the kingdom priorities are. In the kingdom, we are to look to God's reward rather than show off our righteousness so we can receive honor from those around us. In the kingdom, we are to acquire treasures with God rather than amass wealth down here. In the kingdom, we trust God to supply our needs rather than worry about basic requirements like food, drink, and clothing. Kingdom priorities seek God's honor and God's will, and then God himself adds these other things to our lives as needed. This is a verse worth memorizing: "Seek first his kingdom and his righteousness, and all these things will be given to you as well."

EXAMINE

"Each day has enough trouble of its own." These words often come to my mind in their King James form: "Sufficient unto the day is the evil thereof." Certainly there are things we can do to plan ahead for tomorrow. But sometimes there is plenty to deal with today. Sometimes it is a victory to trust in God for the challenges of today, even though great challenges lie ahead tomorrow. After we have done everything we can to stand, we need to let it go and let God do the rest. God will take care of us tomorrow just like he took care of us today. A little sleep might actually make tomorrow better.

EXPLORE

The promise that all these other things will be given to us if we seek God first is not a promise of prosperity, but a promise that God will take care of us if we put him first. At times it can take great trust. Indeed, it is ironic that sometimes God allows us to suffer and be persecuted—it is eternity that is added to us then. But we must put God first no matter what, even if our lives end in persecution and death. God is the most important. Even if he did not provide for us we would be obligated to serve him, whether by choice now or when every knee will bow before him by force later.

PRAYER

Father, help me to see that you come first no matter what. Help me rest in the knowledge that you will provide all I need in any and all circumstances.

The will of God is not something you add to your life. . . . You either line yourself up with the Son of God . . . or you capitulate to the principle which governs the rest of the world.

—ELISABETH ELLIOT

BRIDGING JESUS' WORLD AND OURS

The treasures of the modern world are in some respects the same, in some respects different from those of the ancient world. We live in a different sort of economy. Although many people barely get by, living from hand to mouth, those in the West are incredibly wealthy in comparison to most people in the rest of the world and throughout history. Most Western countries have a "safety net" of welfare that keeps the poor from starving, and there is even public housing available.

It has become easier than ever to lay up treasures on earth without even realizing it. It has become easier than ever to worry about things that are insignificant beyond belief in the light of eternity. We would almost have to lose everything to realize how blessed we are materially in this age.

In this light, how can we align ourselves with kingdom values? How can we ensure that our investments are really in heaven rather than on earth? God will show us if we are willing to listen. He will help us see where our excess might overflow to others and what things on earth we are too attached to.

EXERCISE

Spend this week listening to God, asking him where your treasures are. Could you lose everything and be satisfied in God? What would be hardest to give up? Open yourself up to the Spirit to teach you about yourself and adjust accordingly.

Week 5

AUTHENTIC LOVE
Matthew 7:1–14

So in everything, do to others what you
would have them do to you, for this sums
up the Law and the Prophets.

—MATTHEW 7:12

Day 1

DON'T JUDGE
Matthew 7:1–5

INTRODUCTION

A good deal of Matthew 6 had to do with hypocritical behavior, individuals who pretend to be righteous but are not. Matthew 7 continues this theme.

ENGAGE

A hypocrite is someone who pretends to be something he or she is not. In these verses, Jesus warned the person who criticizes, even condemns, someone else for an area in which he or she is an even worse offender. Like those who need forgiveness but do not forgive, Jesus warned those who need patience or mercy in the very areas that they will not show patience or mercy to others. They have a "plank" in their own eye but are condemning someone who only has a "speck" in his or hers. The imagery may be a little weird to us, but we get the point. We have no business trying to help others with problem areas in which we ourselves are defeated.

By judging others we blind ourselves to our own evil and to the grace which others are just as entitled to as we are.

—DIETRICH BONHOEFFER

EXAMINE

In 1 Corinthians, Paul told the Corinthians that it is not our place to judge others (4:3–5) and then proceeded to judge a member of their assembly (5:3). How do these two fit together? A key difference is that one judgment has to do more with inner motivations. The other has to do with clear actions. The judging we are not to do is twofold. First, we are not to pass judgment on inner, hidden motivations that are not clear. Most of all, we are not to condemn others for things of which we ourselves are actually guilty. But there are other actions, like murder or adultery, whose meanings are clear. It is not "judging" to recognize such things as wrongdoing.

EXPLORE

You may have studied something called projection in a psychology class. Projection is when we see our own faults in others—whether or not they are really there. A wife who is cheating begins to be paranoid about her own husband. She might accuse him of the very thing she is doing. A dishonest worker might distrust others because he himself is not trustworthy. Perhaps a pastor preaches a little too much on a particular topic because he or she may struggle with it. The worst part is that we can project our faults and sins onto others without even realizing it. But if we let the Lord change us in these areas, we will stop judging others too.

PRAYER

Father, please remove all the planks from my eyes so I might see clearly.

Day 2

THOSE WHO REJECT
Matthew 7:6

INTRODUCTION

Matthew 7:6 is a good example of a short saying of Jesus that does not need a context in order to make sense. The verse is usually quoted on its own.

ENGAGE

At least at one time, this saying of Jesus was very familiar. Pearls are something of great value to many people, but a pig cannot appreciate them. Similarly, something that is holy is more than special. It is something God has set apart as his own. You would not give something like that to a dog, remembering that dogs were not seen as "man's best friend" in the ancient world. Not only will pigs and dogs not thank you for such precious items, but they are just as likely to turn on you. Perhaps in these words we can feel Jesus' pain at bringing the tremendous message of the kingdom of God to people who not only did not treasure it, but killed him.

Nothing in the world is more dangerous than
sincere ignorance and conscientious stupidity.

—MARTIN LUTHER KING, JR.

EXAMINE

It is so easy to listen to a thousand words going in a direction we do not like, only to throw them all away by focusing on one word we do want to hear. So after reading Jesus' many words about loving our enemy and going the second mile, we might hear this saying and throw his more basic message away. We become elitist: "I would share my knowledge with you, but you are not worth it"; "I am better than you, and you are not worth my effort." Perhaps the key in practice is to be very slow to think it is useless to continue sharing the good news with someone. Perhaps we should never even entertain the possibility until we have been trampled a little.

EXPLORE

God gives us the choice. He will not make us love the holy. And his pearls will do us no good unless we are open to them. Perhaps there are things we believe that are pointless to share with those who do not. But we should never give up on the possibility that a dog might change, even as we show wisdom in sharing the jewels of the kingdom with them. For everything there is a season. There is a time to share and there is a time to wipe the dust off our feet and move on.

PRAYER

Spirit, give me the wisdom to recognize and relish the holy. Give me discernment on when to share the jewels of the kingdom.

Day 3

ASK, SEEK, KNOCK
Matthew 7:7–8

INTRODUCTION

In its own way, these verses continue the theme that we do not need to worry because God will take care of us. We can ask him for what we need.

ENGAGE

This passage tells us that we have a God who wants to help us. He is a God who wants to answer when we call. He is a God who wants to be found when we seek him. He is a God who wants to open doors for us. He is not a God who cannot be bothered with our needs. He is not a distant God we have to beg to pay us attention. He does not make us jump through hoops to get an appointment. We do not have to bug him over and over before he will do anything. This promise is to "every-one," not just a select few he has chosen. God is an equal opportunity answerer.

When you ask, you do not receive, because you ask with wrong motives, that you may spend what you get on your pleasures.

—JAMES 4:3

EXAMINE

God is not a genie who grants us all our wishes. Even though Jesus said it boldly—"Ask and it will be given to you"—he was using ordinary language. He did not mean, "Ask for your neighbor to have a heart attack, and I have you covered." Our requests must be in sync with his heart and his will. Even the Holy Spirit intercedes for us in accordance with God's will (Rom. 8:27). When we are in sync with him, we pray, "if the Lord wills" (James 4:15). When our hearts are right with God, we will ask for the right sorts of things. We will not ask selfishly or for evil. And we will ask in submission to God's master plan.

EXPLORE

Believing that God is near us can sometimes be a matter of faith. Sometimes we do not feel like he has answered. Sometimes we do not feel like he is anywhere to be found or that he has opened the door on which we have been knocking. An answer of "no" on a specific request may be because he is saying "yes" to a much greater good. Sometimes we feel like we are unable to find him, because he is deepening our faith. At other times he is pushing us to rely on each other. At still other times he is correcting our misunderstanding of what finding him means. Finally, sometimes we are only pretending to seek him and are really trying not to find him.

PRAYER

Father, I believe you are answering. Give me the strength not to be discouraged when it does not feel that way.

Day 4

THE GOLDEN RULE
Matthew 7:9–12

INTRODUCTION

These verses help clarify the kinds of requests that yesterday's verses were talking about. The asking that God answers is the asking that has to do with our true needs. God gives us the things we really need.

ENGAGE

In these verses, Jesus pictured the typical father, the one who desperately wants to feed his children. Fathers are meant to model for their children what their heavenly Father is like. Those who grow up with an absent or abusive father often struggle to have an accurate picture of God. They may have a skewed sense of God without even knowing it. If a father is violent and unpredictable, it will be hard for his children to believe that God is good or to be trusted. It is a sacred task to be a father or mother. If we are not like the father or mother Jesus assumes is typical here, we need to change.

*Whoever thinks they understand the Holy Scriptures,
any part of them, but interprets them in a way
that does not tend to build up the twofold love
of God and our neighbor, they do not yet
understand the Scriptures as they should.*

—AUGUSTINE

EXAMINE

Matthew 7:12 is the Golden Rule, and it gives us another way of understanding the law of love. For Jesus, Paul, and the whole New Testament, the command to love our neighbor and enemy is the whole law (see, for example, Matt. 22:37–39; Rom. 13:8–10). Any attempt to apply the Bible outside this law of love is a misapplication. Act toward others the way you would want others to treat you. Most of us would not want someone to kill us or steal from us, so we should not do these things to other people either. It is quite possible that this verse is meant to close the section that began with Jesus saying he came to fulfill the Law and the Prophets.

EXPLORE

Some of us do not really expect good from God. Some of us think of God like a sheriff who is just waiting for us to break the law. I had this problem in my youth. What if I could not remember everything I had done wrong? Would God forgive me if I did not specifically confess every single sin? God is not such an accountant. His love is prodigal. He wants to forgive us. He is longing for us to give him an excuse to forgive. If we suffer, it is not because he is teaching us a lesson in a punitive sense, but because something bigger is going on or perhaps because he wants to make us better people.

PRAYER

Father, help me to see clearly what a good father is, and then let me never doubt that you are the best Father there could ever be.

Day 5

THE NARROW GATE
Matthew 7:13–14

INTRODUCTION

These verses arguably begin the closing section of the sermon. Jesus has given extensive teaching on what it means to fulfill the Jewish Law. He has given many examples of true righteousness. Now, who will listen?

ENGAGE

We like to think that it was obvious at the time to anyone around that Jesus was the Messiah. We like to focus on lots of crowds following Jesus. But in the vast scheme of things, it was just a small portion of Israel. After Jesus rose from the dead, Acts tells us that thousands believed and the word began to spread. But, again, this was a small portion of the overall populace. By the 50s, when Paul wrote Romans, he struggled with the fact that most of the Jews did not accept Jesus (for example, Rom. 9:27). Eventually, Christianity would become an overwhelmingly non-Jewish phenomenon, although only a small percentage of Gentiles believed. Narrow is the road that leads to life.

EXAMINE

A self-fulfilling prophecy occurs when we help make something happen because we expect it to happen. So, if you do not expect many people to get right with God, you may not try very hard, and, as a result, not many people may get right with God. No matter whether we think many or few will be in the kingdom of God, we must live as though everyone could make it. We also have to be careful not to get an elitist attitude, thinking that we are part of some special, privileged few. Outcasts from society can develop this attitude as a defense mechanism. But at other times, we can get the kind of superiority complex that Jesus condemned in Matthew 6.

EXPLORE

Until recent times, most people in America have thought of themselves as Christians. From the time when Christianity became the only legal religion of the Roman Empire, almost all of Europe and its colonies became Christian, at least in name. As we know, however, not everyone who claims to be a Christ-follower truly is. How many people are truly virtuous? How many people are unselfish and almost always try to do the right thing? Even our churches are full of people who go through the motions but do not really submit to the King. Jesus may not have been making a statement about all time, but it is sobering to wonder if even most of those who call themselves Christians today are actually on the road to destruction.

PRAYER

Spirit, guide my feet on the narrow path. Keep me from straying into the easy way that ends in destruction.

I am a fool for Christ. . . . Whose fool are you?

—BROTHER ANDREW

BRIDGING JESUS' WORLD AND OURS

The teaching of Jesus in the first part of Matthew 7 is just as applicable to us today as it ever was. Each bit of teaching is a snapshot that needs to be balanced with other snapshots. We are not to judge others when we cannot see their motives, but at the same time we should not cast God's pearls in front of swine. We should feel free to ask God for anything, but God does not always answer our prayers in the way we want. God is always to be found but not always in the place we want to find him.

Nevertheless, God is always there, waiting to be found, waiting to be asked. He shows us not only what a perfect father looks like but how we should treat others. The Golden Rule really cuts to the chase in how we are to live with our neighbors and enemies. Would we want others to do to us what we do to them? Would we want others to judge us in the way we judge them?

EXERCISE

Every time this week you feel tempted to criticize or condemn someone, stop and examine yourself. Are there any instances in your life where you are guilty of the very same thing or something similar? Ask God to change your attitudes as necessary.

Week 6

BUILDING YOUR HOUSE
Matthew 7:15–29

Therefore everyone who hears these words of mine
and puts them into practice is like a wise man who
built his house on the rock. The rain came down,
the streams rose, and the winds blew and beat
against that house; yet it did not fall.

—MATTHEW 7:24–25

Day 1

FALSE PROPHETS
Matthew 7:15–16

INTRODUCTION

If few are actually on the right path, how can we tell who is actually on the narrow path and who is on the broad path to destruction? The key is the fruit in the lives of those who claim to speak for God.

ENGAGE

Wolves in sheep's clothing is a familiar image. Someone looks like a good person, a friend, but it turns out they mean you harm. They are not your friend. They are out for themselves or at least something quite different from how they first represented themselves. Even "Satan himself masquerades as an angel of light" (2 Cor. 11:14). It can take discernment to know when you are really looking at a wolf. Jesus said their fruit is the best indicator. Sometimes it can take a while to see the fruit. Sometimes we can spot inconsistencies. So we walk the tightrope between not wanting to judge others and being able to discern a wolf in sheep's clothing.

Dear friends, do not believe every spirit, but test the spirits to see whether they are from God, because many false prophets have gone out into the world.

—1 JOHN 4:1

EXAMINE

Prophecy was a major element of the early church. When Ephesians says that the church was built on the foundation of the apostles and prophets (Eph. 2:20; see also 2 Pet. 3:2), it probably referred to the prophets of the New Testament period. We have the New Testament today, but for the first decades after Christ, a good deal had to be figured out. God not only used the apostles to guide the early church, but also prophets. Some, however, misguided the church (see 1 John 4:1). Traveling teachers were apparently a major problem, especially after the first apostles began to fade from the scene. This paragraph in Matthew 7 may address such individuals who talked a good talk but whose life betrayed the truth about them.

EXPLORE

The problem with discerning wolves is that they look an awful lot like sheep. In a context where the Bible is the standard of truth, they will come to you quoting verses. If you live in a community where the Spirit is very important, they will come to you with revelations from the Spirit. If you worship in a community that follows historical traditions, they will attend the right services, wear the right clothing, and do the right ritual. Perhaps the best counterbalance is the body of Christ. What does the community as a whole think? What do the most spiritually discerning people in your fellowship think? What do outsiders think? Where have these teachers been before and what were their fruits there?

PRAYER

Spirit, give me your eyes to see what you see. Raise up true prophets among us so we can discern the false ones.

Day 2

THE RIGHT FRUIT
Matthew 7:17–20

INTRODUCTION

Jesus continued to talk about good and bad trees and the kinds of fruit we would expect to come from each. These verses end with his repeating the truth that we know a tree by its fruit.

ENGAGE

The kind of fruit to which Jesus referred is the fruit of a good life. He had been talking about good fruit throughout the sermon. The Beatitudes mention good fruit—being a peacemaker, being merciful, and hungering for righteousness, for example. Good fruit in the rest of Matthew 5 includes loving our enemies and being truthful. Good fruit in Matthew 6 involves a life that is lived to honor God, not to get honor from others. It involves trusting him for its needs. Then, in the first part of Matthew 7, we learn that good fruit does not judge others in relation to its own faults. We bear good fruit when we look to God for help and do to others what we would have them do to us.

The fruit of the Spirit is love, joy, peace, forbearance, kindness, goodness, faithfulness, gentleness and self-control. Against such things there is no law.

—GALATIANS 5:22–23

EXAMINE

Unfortunately, a climate has developed in Christianity that expects Christians to look more or less just like those who do not believe: "I'm not perfect, just forgiven." This notion stands in strong contrast to what Jesus said in these verses. A good tree, he said, brings forth good fruit. A tree that does not bear good fruit needs to be cut down; that sort of tree is thrown into the fire. The allusion to hell is clear, especially given how often Matthew alludes to hellfire. "A bad tree bears bad fruit." Sometimes, to be sure, we produce mixed fruit. But God is very good with trees. He knows just how to turn around a tree in trouble and cultivate good fruit.

EXPLORE

It is easy to do the right thing when we live in a comfortable environment where we are loved, have everything we need, and are rewarded for doing the right thing. We do not all come from such a place. There are believers who live among weeds that make bearing good fruit a constant struggle. God has only love and support for those who are struggling with all their might to live Jesus' way. But we should also beware of making excuses for ourselves, a constant human tendency: "I wouldn't normally have had that fruit, but . . ." It is still bad fruit, and the bottom line remains the same: "Every good tree bears good fruit."

PRAYER

Spirit, open my eyes to see any bad fruit on my tree for what it is. Prune me until the tree is good to the root.

Day 3

A BAD SURPRISE
Matthew 7:21–23

INTRODUCTION

These verses end Jesus' paragraph on false prophets
and on knowing true ambassadors of Christ by their fruit.
Some may be surprised on the day of judgment to find
that they have not made it into the kingdom.

ENGAGE

It may be a little shocking to hear that some Christian
leaders in the early church were not really Christians.
How sobering these words in Matthew must have been to
their first audiences as well! "Lord, did we not prophesy
in your name?" How many preachers today may find out
on the last day that their hearts were not truly with God?
"Did we not perform many miracles in your name?"

How many high-profile Christians put on a show, maybe even see real miracles take place, but are not really with Christ? In the end, it is not about the power, and it is not about the knowledge. It is about knowing Christ and seeing the fruit in our lives.

Many false prophets will appear
and deceive many people.

—MATTHEW 24:11

EXAMINE

This is not the only passage in Matthew where we get a strong feeling that not everyone who called him- or herself a Christian in the early church really was one. The parable of the weeds in Matthew 13 tells us that God has let "weeds" grow alongside the "wheat" until the day of judgment, when it all will be sorted and the weeds will be burned. The parable of the sheep and the goats in Matthew 25 similarly tells of many individuals who will be surprised to join the Devil and his angels in hell because they did not show love to those in need when they had the opportunity. As the preceding verses have shown, true followers bear good fruit.

EXPLORE

The church has developed its own kind of Pharisee, individuals who have learned how to put on a Christian show. Some know how to preach and present the Word of the Lord. Some know how to perform miracles. Some know how to cast out demons. Some know how to show up on Sunday morning for church. Some know how to look very respectable, give 10 percent of their income, and avoid all the wrong places. But the real deal is a matter of the heart, not externals or a show. It is a heart that is truly oriented around God and his kingdom. It is a heart that reaches out to others to help in a time of need.

PRAYER

Lord, do not let me fool myself into thinking I am your servant if in fact I am only living for myself.

Day 4

WISE BUILDERS
Matthew 7:24–27

INTRODUCTION

Many of us know the words of the childhood song: "The wise man built his house upon the rock." But they are actually a fitting conclusion to the whole Sermon on the Mount. The wise person builds on rock by listening to Jesus' teaching.

ENGAGE

Those who build their house on rock are the people who hear Jesus' words in the sermon and put them into practice. These are the people who enter through the narrow gate and follow the narrow path. These are the people are completely like our heavenly Father, who go the second mile and not only love their friends, but their enemies as well. These are the people who treat others the way they would like others to treat them. These are the people who turn the other cheek and lay up treasures for themselves in heaven. These are the people who have removed the planks from their eyes so their eyes are full of light and see the world like God sees it.

The loftier the building, the deeper the foundation must be laid.

—THOMAS À KEMPIS

EXAMINE

A house might seem like a pretty sturdy thing, but watch what happens when a river overflows its banks in a flood or a tsunami hits. What happens when a sink-hole suddenly appears underneath? Sometimes even a misplaced trickle over time can erode a foundation. Then the whole house, heavy though it is, may flow down the river or tumble to the ground. The foolish person in this parable refers to those who accumulate treasures on earth, those who either try to store their excess or who worry too much about earthly things. These are people who go halfway with the letter of the law but do not keep its spirit. They follow the wide road that leads to destruction.

EXPLORE

What are you going to do with the Sermon on the Mount? If you have grown up in church, you probably have heard most of its teaching at some point or another. Familiarity can inoculate us from a truth or idea. Some of the sermon is really hard to put into practice: "How can I stop worrying about food and clothing if I am truly destitute?" "How can I love my enemy when he or she has mistreated me so badly?" Thankfully, God does not ask us to do it alone. Not only do we have his Holy Spirit to help, but we also have each other in the body of Christ. We do not have to build the house alone.

PRAYER

Jesus, build my house with me. I long for your instruction on building sites and materials. I long for your help.

Day 5

AMAZING AUTHORITY
Matthew 7:28–29

INTRODUCTION

After the sermon was over, the crowds were in awe of Jesus' teaching. He did not present options and conflicting points of view; he told it just like it was, with authority.

ENGAGE

The introduction to this devotional noted the fact that Jesus gave this sermon on a mountain, like Moses received the law on a mountain. When we looked at Jesus fulfilling the law in Matthew 5, we thought of Moses as the one through whom God gave the law to Israel. Like Moses, an important political figure tried to kill Jesus as a child. And like Moses, Jesus emerged from Egypt. Here, the crowds observed the authority with which Jesus taught his fulfilled law. He is the new Moses, the one through whom God was giving the new covenant. But this time, God was not just giving the law to Israel. He was showing the way for all people.

EXAMINE

In education today, a person who merely indoctrinates is not considered a good teacher. A good teacher is considered to be someone who teaches students to think on their own so that they can continue to think well after the teacher is no longer there to tell them the answers. So a good teacher usually presents the various options and presents them fairly. Students then get to decide what they think. Suffice it to say, Jesus did not teach this way. Jesus taught with authority. He gave the right answers. He *did* expect the people to adopt his teaching and squarely told them that their houses would crumble if they did not follow him. No wonder the crowds were amazed!

EXPLORE

Do we have the same authority today to proclaim the truth as Jesus did? Certainly we can pass on Jesus' own words with the authority they have on their own. That is not our authority but *his* authority we are conveying. As we do so, we should remember the proverbial nature of his teaching and that he gave more than one angle on many topics. We should also make sure we fully understand what God was saying in Scripture when we proclaim it. Sometimes a preacher will authoritatively present a misunderstanding or some tradition he or she has inherited. But there is a time when the Spirit is with you and you know you have authority to speak a word from the Lord.

PRAYER

Spirit, do not let me speak authoritatively when I do not understand, but also do not let me speak feebly an authoritative word.

*Christ now occupies the supreme seat of
cosmic authority. The kings of this world and
all secular governments may ignore this
reality, but they cannot undo it.*

—R. C. Sproul

BRIDGING JESUS' WORLD AND OURS

It is a tremendous burden to realize the impact we can have in the world for both good and evil. If we are serving the Lord, we should not worry about being on the broad path to destruction or about potentially being a false prophet. Such individuals do not open themselves up to the voice of the Lord. They hardly give a thought to whether *they* might be guilty of the same things of which they so happily accuse others.

It is especially important that we not try to walk that path alone. Alone, we are more prone not to see the planks in our eyes. Alone, we are more likely to be self-deceived. Alone, we can mistake the voice in our head for the voice of Jesus. How much better to hear that we are on the wrong path from a concerned brother or sister than to hear the Lord tell us on the final day that he never knew us!

EXERCISE

In the next week, read through the entire Sermon on the Mount again, maybe even more than once. Try to read it at least once in a single sitting. Are you building your house on solid rock? If the sermon were a checklist, how many of the boxes have you checked? Which ones still need your attention?

Life Lessons from Key Moments of Jesus' Life

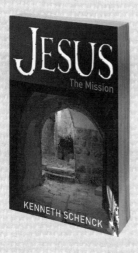
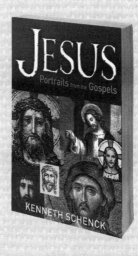

New Testament scholar Kenneth Schenck bridges time and culture to bring you *Jesus—The Mission* and *Jesus—Portraits from the Gospels*. Immerse yourself in the world of history's most transformative figure and see his life, message, mission, ministry, and miracles from the lens of those who knew him best. These are not just history books; each chapter concludes with the author's reflections about how Jesus' life and mission shape our lives more into his image.

Jesus—The Mission
ISBN: 978-0-89827-674-9
eBook: 978-0-89827-675-6

Jesus—Portraits from the Gospels
ISBN: 978-0-89827-676-3
eBook: 978-0-89827-677-0

Deeper Devotions on the Life of Christ

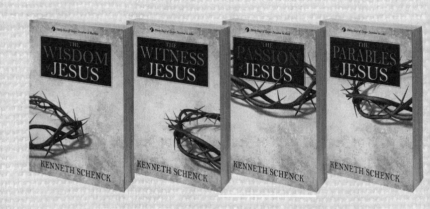

Join New Testament scholar Kenneth Schenck as he reflects deeply on the life and ministry of Jesus recorded in the Gospels.

Based on the solid scholarship found in Schenck's two books, *Jesus—The Mission* and *Jesus—Portraits from the Gospels*, these books each provide thirty days of in-depth devotions on Jesus. Each devotion will challenge you to engage, examine, and explore another aspect of Jesus' life and then take it to God in prayer.

The Wisdom of Jesus
ISBN: 978-0-89827-739-5
eBook: 978-0-89827-816-3

The Witness of Jesus
ISBN: 978-0-89827-740-1
eBook: 978-0-89827-817-0

The Passion of Jesus
ISBN: 978-0-89827-737-1
eBook: 978-0-89827-814-9

The Parables of Jesus
ISBN: 978-0-89827-738-8
eBook: 978-0-89827-815-6